praying like JESUS

written by
KENDRA ANDRUS

illustrated by
SORINEL CÂRSTIUC

Author's Note:
The rainbow imagery in this book symbolizes
God's beautiful promise of presence and goodness, as well as the truth
that we are connected to God through prayer —
a bridge from us to heaven, and from heaven to us.

For

Wally

Beloved Nephew,

*May your prayers carry you higher
and empower you to change the world!*

Daddy of everyone,
You are the King of Heaven.

The place where You live is perfect and there is
no hurt or sadness or anything bad there.

Our Father, Who art in Heaven

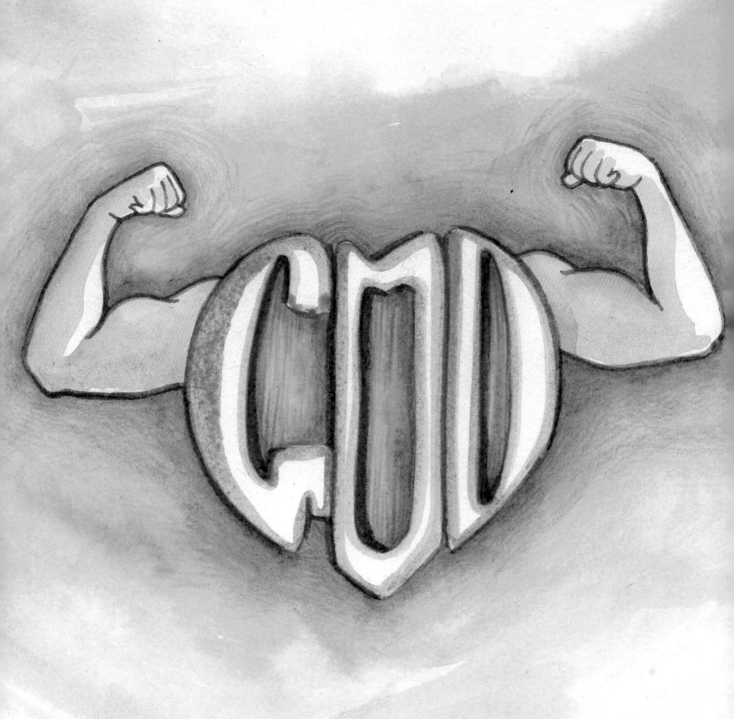

Your name is GREAT!
Your name is bigger and stronger
than any other name.

You are different and better than
anyone or anything on this earth!

Hallowed be Thy name

Please send the goodness of Your heart to us.
Please cover up the badness here with Your love.

Please move into my heart
and make Your home in me,
so I can carry You with me everywhere.

Thy Kingdom come

Please help us to love You
and follow Your ways.

Please help us to see with Your eyes
and hear with Your ears.

Thy will be done

Please make this world a different and better place —

and use us to do it.

On Earth as it is in Heaven

Please give us everything we need for each day.

Give us food for our bellies so we can grow strong and stay healthy...

Give us knowledge for our brains so we can be smart
and give us wisdom to make good decisions.

Give us confidence in our hearts so that we can be
brave and know that we are valuable and important
and loved.

Give us this day our daily bread

And forgive us when we make bad choices
and are sorry for them.

Help us to forgive others who hurt us
because of Your great love for everyone.

Keep us free from anger and the desire
to hurt people back.

And forgive us our trespasses as we forgive those who

trespass against us.

Do not let us go places
that will harm us or confuse us.

Help us to stay away from people who
try to get us to do bad things.

When we hear things that are not
what You say, please plug our ears.

And lead us not into temptation

Rescue us from the dungeon
of fear and anger and shame.

Never let us believe in lies.

But deliver us from evil

For You have the keys
to Life and Heaven!

Only You are the strongest!

Only You are the best!

For Thine is the Kingdom, the power...

You can do anything
and I cheer for You always!

...and the glory forever!

This is what my heart really wants!
This is all true and good. Forever.

I LOVE YOU, GOD!

AMEN!

the
end

amen!
amen!

About the Author

Kendra Andrus is a homeschooling mother who finds endless inspiration for children's books in her everyday life with her own six children. She writes to solve their problems, answer their questions, and tell the stories of their adventures together. She loves Jesus, teaching, cooking, reading, art, poetry, dancing, and singing. Together, she and her husband manage the loud and feisty-fun chaos that is their daily life in Nashville, Tennessee.

About the Illustrator

Sorinel Cârstiuc graduated from the University of Fine Arts in Iasi, Romania. He is currently a professor at the Art High School "Hadirclea Darclee" in Braila, Romania. He founded the "Bellart Atelier Creativ," a workshop for children and teens. He has participated in many art projects and exhibitions.

Made in the USA
Middletown, DE
11 December 2018